From Your Friends at The MAILBOX®

I CAN MAKE IT!
I CAN READ IT!

20 Reproducible Booklets to Develop Early Literacy Skills

SPRING

WRITTEN BY:
Nancy Anderson, Linda Morgason, Jan Robbins

EDITED BY:
Mary Lester
Kim T. Griswell

ILLUSTRATED BY:
Pam Crane, Sheila Krill, Mary Lester, Kimberly Richard

COVER DESIGN BY:
Nick Greenwood and Kimberly Richard

www.themailbox.com

Manufactured in the United States
10 9 8 7 6 5 4 3 2 1

TABLE OF CONTENTS

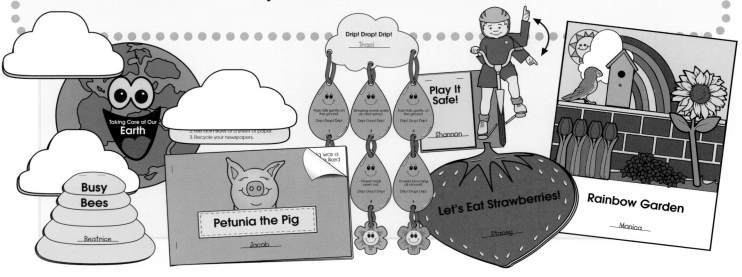

TALE OF A KITE

Reading skills will soar to new heights with this kite booklet! Give each student a copy of pages 4–6. Then have each student color his booklet cover and booklet illustrations. Instruct the student to cut out his booklet cover, page, and illustrations along the bold outer lines. Help him cut slits along the dotted lines on the booklet cover. Next, encourage him to apply a thin line of glue along the gray area of the booklet page. Then direct him to align the cover on top of the booklet page and press. Have him glue the illustrations to the back of the booklet as shown. When the glue has dried, help him fold back the illustrations so they do not show. Read a completed booklet with students, demonstrating how to unfold the appropriate illustration as each page is read. Provide time for each student to practice reading with a partner before taking his booklet home to read to family members.

CREATIVE DECORATING OPTION

- Give each student a 12-inch length of colorful yarn and four 6-inch pieces of contrasting yarn. Punch a hole at the bottom of the booklet and tie one end of the 12-inch yarn to it. Then tie the shorter pieces to the kite tail.

Tale of a Kite

Tale of Ki

"I am free!" said Little Kite. She waved her tail as she sailed into the sky.

Char Na

Extend this booklet activity by reading to students *Crosby* by Dennis Haseley (Harcourt Brace & Company, 1996).

Booklet Cover

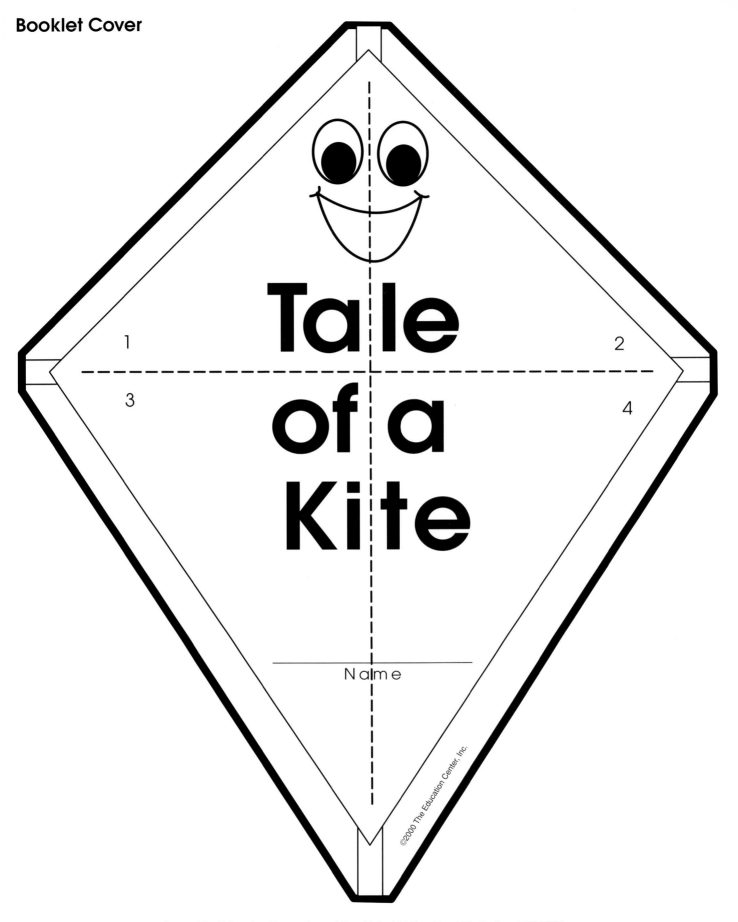

Tale of a Kite

1

2

3

4

Name

©2000 The Education Center, Inc. • *I Can Make It! I Can Read It!* • *Spring* • TEC3507

4 **Note to the teacher:** Use with "Tale of a Kite" on page 3.

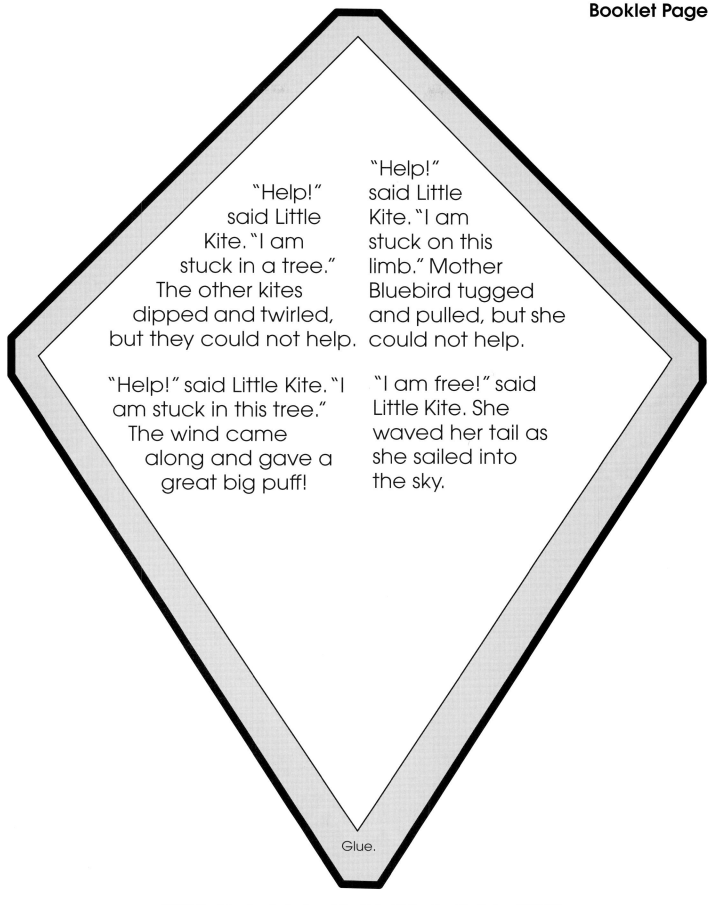

"Help!" said Little Kite. "I am stuck in a tree." The other kites dipped and twirled, but they could not help.

"Help!" said Little Kite. "I am stuck in this tree." The wind came along and gave a great big puff!

"Help!" said Little Kite. "I am stuck on this limb." Mother Bluebird tugged and pulled, but she could not help.

"I am free!" said Little Kite. She waved her tail as she sailed into the sky.

Glue.

Note to the teacher: Use with "Tale of a Kite" on page 3.

Booklet Illustrations

Glue behind flap 1.

Glue behind flap 2.

Glue behind flap 3.

Glue behind flap 4.

Note to the teacher: Use with "Tale of a Kite" on page 3.

LUNCHBOX OF A SUPERHERO

Serve your young heroes and heroines the nutritious facts about healthy foods with this informational booklet! Give each student a copy of pages 9–12, a construction paper copy of page 8, and a brad. Instruct each student to color his pages. Have him cut out the booklet backing, cover, and pages; then have him punch holes at the top of each where indicated. Next, direct the student to stack his pages in numerical order, placing the cover on top and the backing on the bottom. Staple the pages together at the bottom of the booklet as shown. Help him insert the brad through the booklet to secure his lunchbox. When the projects have been completed, remove the brad from one and read it with students. Then provide time for each student to practice reading his booklet with a partner. When students have had sufficient practice, have them secure their lunchboxes with their brads. Encourage students to take their booklets home to read to family members. Reading this booklet will be a tasty treat!

CREATIVE DECORATING OPTION

• Glue magazine pictures of food to the last page of the booklet.

Extend this booklet activity by having each student keep a diary of the food he eats in one day. Then encourage the student to check his booklet to determine how healthy his diet was.

Lunchbox of a Superhero

Sean
Name

Booklet Backing and Cover

Backing

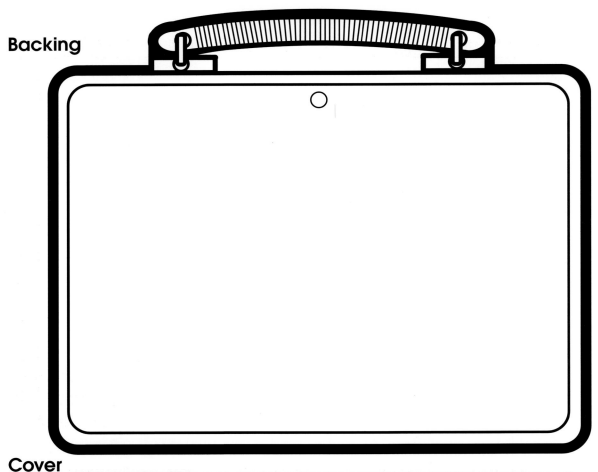

Cover

Lunchbox of a Superhero

_____
Name

I need to eat healthy food every day. Healthy food makes my body strong.

1

To be healthy, I need 6 to 11 servings of the bread, cereal, rice, and pasta group every day.

bread

cereal

rice

pasta

2

Note to the teacher: Use with "Lunchbox of a Superhero" on page 7.

To be healthy, I need two to three servings of the milk, yogurt, and cheese group every day.

milk

yogurt

cheese

3

To be healthy, I need two to four servings of the fruit group every day.

apples

strawberries

4

Note to the teacher: Use with "Lunchbox of a Superhero" on page 7.

To be healthy, I need three to
five servings of the vegetable
group every day.

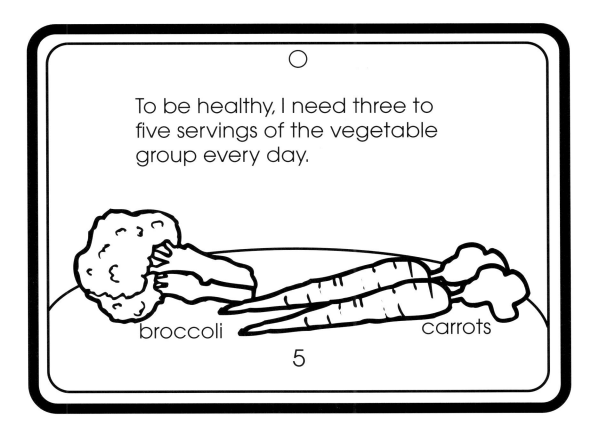

broccoli   carrots

5

To be healthy, I need two to three
servings of the meat, poultry, fish, dry
bean, egg, and nut group every day.

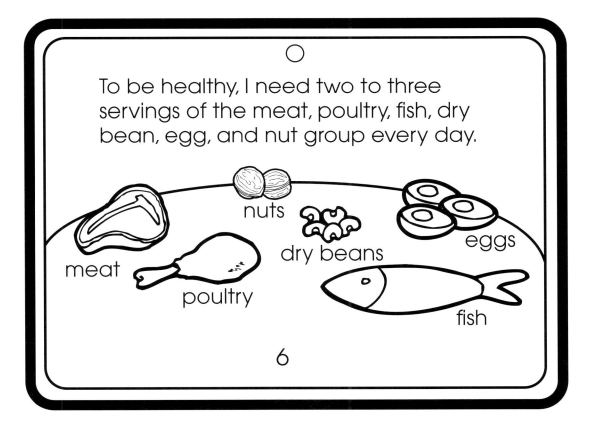

nuts

meat   dry beans   eggs

poultry   fish

6

Note to the teacher: Use with "Lunchbox of a Superhero" on page 7.

To be healthy, I need only a little bit of fats, oils, and sweets every day.

oil

sweets

7

To have a healthy body, I eat food that is good for me!

8

Note to the teacher: Use with "Lunchbox of a Superhero" on page 7.

FEEL THE BEAT!

Your youngsters will be rockin' and readin' with this music booklet! Give each student a copy of pages 14–18. Have each student color his cover and booklet pages. (Remind students to color lightly over the text so the booklet can be read.) Then instruct the student to cut out his cover and booklet pages on the bold outer lines. With his pages in numerical order, have him glue the pages where indicated to create one long strip. When the glue has dried, help him accordion-fold the pages as shown. Then read a completed booklet with students. Encourage each student to practice reading his booklet with a partner before taking it home to read to family members.

CREATIVE DECORATING OPTIONS

- Draw a picture of a musical instrument on the cover.
- Outline the cover's staff with glitter glue.

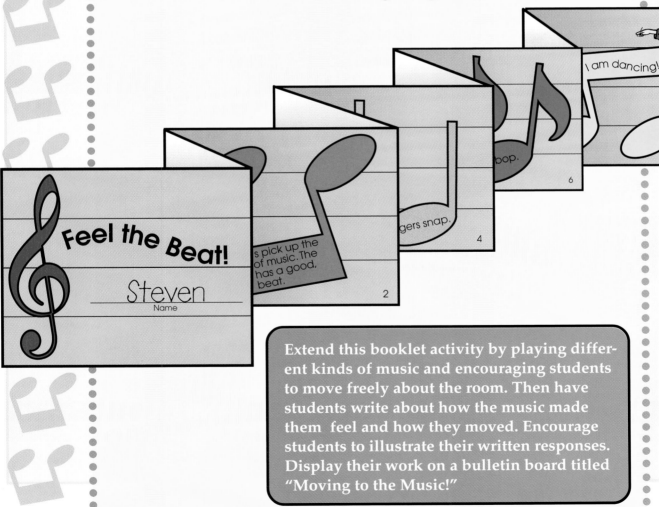

Extend this booklet activity by playing different kinds of music and encouraging students to move freely about the room. Then have students write about how the music made them feel and how they moved. Encourage students to illustrate their written responses. Display their work on a bulletin board titled "Moving to the Music!"

Booklet Cover and Page

Cover

Feel the Beat!

_____
Name

Page

Glue.

From the top of my head to the tips of my toes, my body loves to move to the music!

1

Note to the teacher: Use with "Feel the Beat!" on page 13.

My ears pick up the sound of music. The music has a good, strong beat.

Glue.

2

A good feeling starts to grow inside me and my head bobs to the beat.

Glue.

3

Note to the teacher: Use with "Feel the Beat!" on page 13.

Booklet Pages

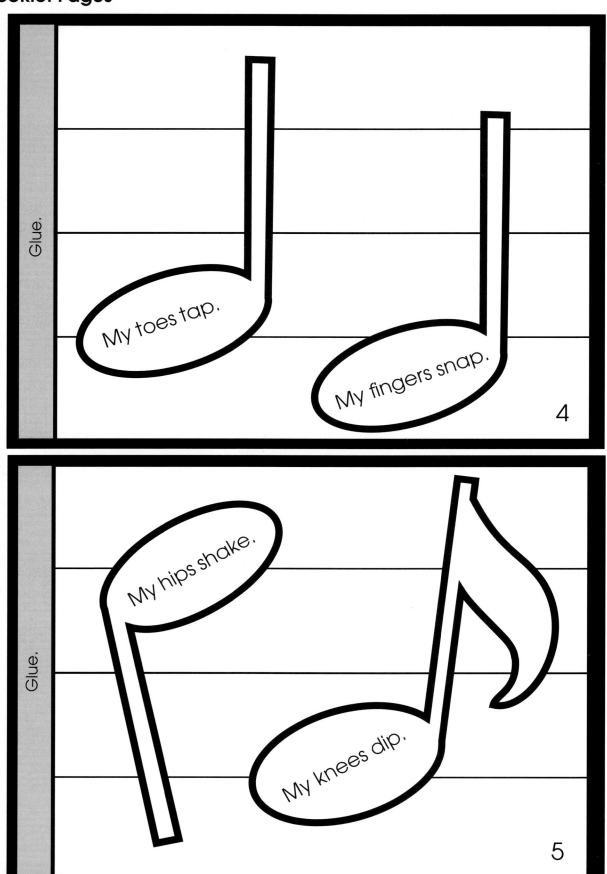

Note to the teacher: Use with "Feel the Beat!" on page 13.

6

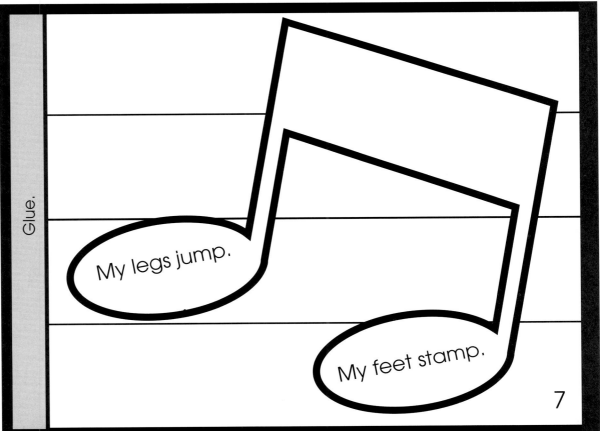

7

Note to the teacher: Use with "Feel the Beat!" on page 13.

©2000 The Education Center, Inc. • *I Can Make It! I Can Read It!* • *Spring* • TEC3507

18 Note to the teacher: Use with "*Feel the Beat!*" on page 13.

BABY BIRDS

Watch your youngsters twitter with excitement as they make and read this delightful rhyming booklet! Give each student a light blue construction paper copy of pages 20–22. Instruct the student to cut out the booklet backing and pages on the bold outer lines. Next, have him stack his pages in numerical order, placing the cover on top. Staple the pages to the backing where indicated. Then read a completed booklet with students. Provide time for each student to practice reading with a buddy. Encourage students to take their booklets home to read to family members and friends. What better place is there to read than at home, "tweet" home?

CREATIVE DECORATING OPTIONS

- Use the backing as a template to trace the outline of the bird onto drawing paper. Cut out the resulting shape and draw an illustration of the story. Staple the drawing to the back of the booklet.
- Outline the bird beak and eye with glitter glue.

Extend this booklet activity by following a hungry cat around the backyard in search of lunch. Read to students *Feathers for Lunch* by Lois Ehlert (Harcourt Brace & Company, 1990).

Baby Birds

Scott
Name

Booklet Backing

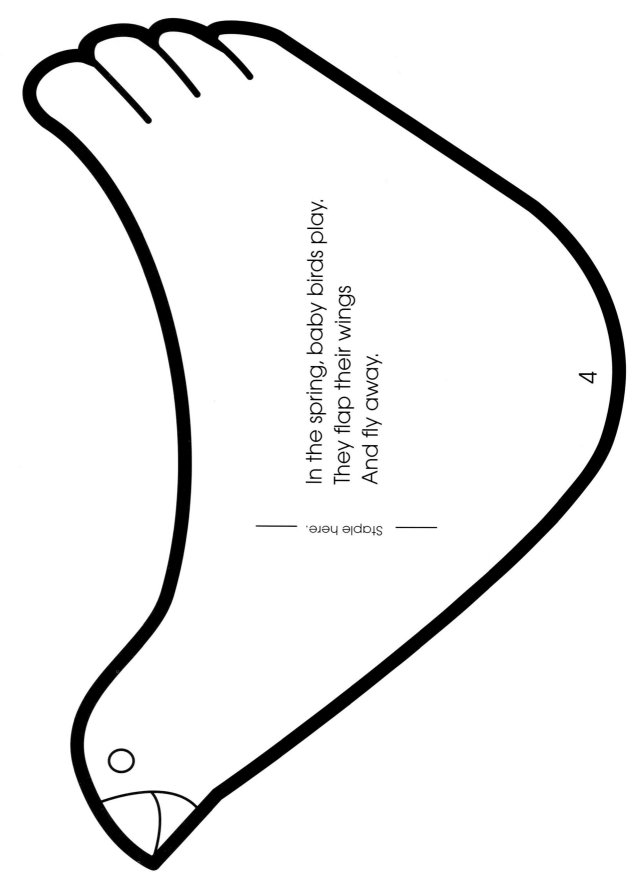

In the spring, baby birds play.
They flap their wings
And fly away.

——— Staple here. ———

4

Cover

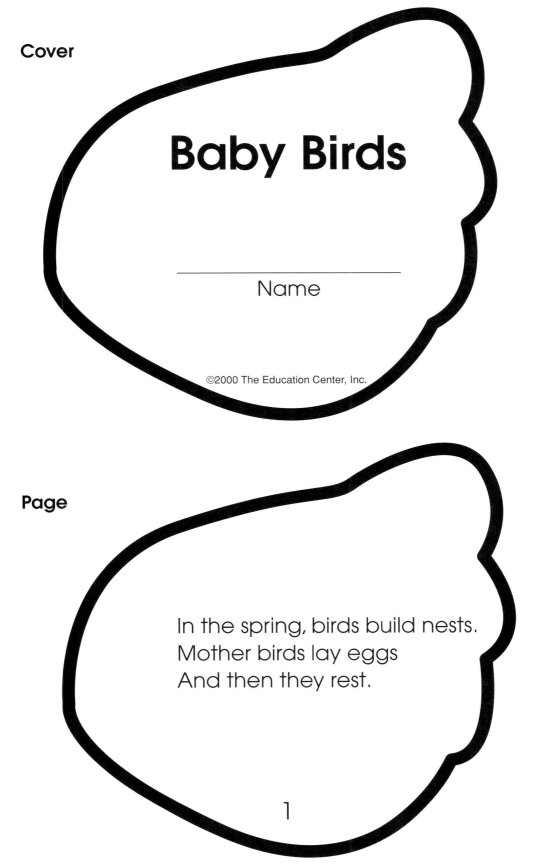

Baby Birds

_____

Name

©2000 The Education Center, Inc.

Page

In the spring, birds build nests.
Mother birds lay eggs
And then they rest.

1

Booklet Pages

In the spring, baby birds hatch.
They eat worms and bugs
Their fathers catch.

2

In the spring, baby birds peep.
They tuck their heads
And try to sleep.

3

Note to the teacher: Use with "Baby Birds" on page 19.

MY RIDDLE BOOK OF ANIMALS

Youngsters will love taking a crack at the animal riddles in this "egg-ceptional" booklet! Give each student a copy of pages 25–28 and a construction paper copy of page 24. Have the student color her illustrations and cut out her booklet covers and pages along the bold outer lines. To cover the answer to the riddle, direct the student to fold each booklet page forward where indicated. Next, have her stack her pages in random order, placing the front cover on top and the back cover on the bottom. Staple the booklet at the left-hand side. Then read a completed booklet with students. Provide time for each student to read her booklet with a buddy before taking it home to read to family members.

CREATIVE DECORATING OPTION

- Using a small sponge and liquid tempera paint, dab paint around the edges of the cover to create a dappled egg.

> Extend this booklet activity by having each student create a riddle about another animal that hatches from an egg, such as an ostrich or penguin. Instruct the student to write her riddle on the front of her back cover and the answer on its back. Then invite each student to read her riddle to the class and have classmates guess the answer.

I have no arms or legs. I am long and thin. I am quiet when I move along the ground. I eat rats and mice. What am I?

I am a sn

Front Cover

My Riddle Book
of Animals

_____
Name

Can you guess the animals that
come from eggs?

Back Cover

©2000 The Education Center, Inc.

©2000 The Education Center, Inc. • _I Can Make It! I Can Read It!_ • _Spring_ • TEC3507

24   **Note to the teacher:** Use with "My Riddle Book of Animals" on page 23.

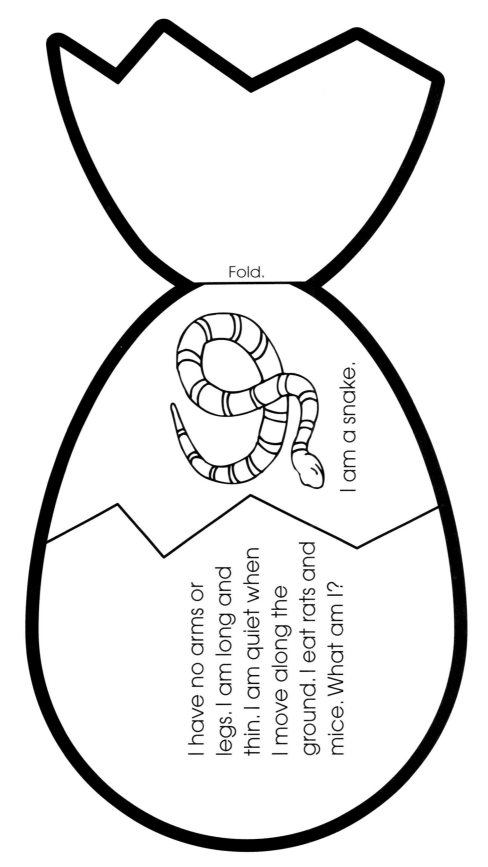

Fold.

I am a snake.

I have no arms or legs. I am long and thin. I am quiet when I move along the ground. I eat rats and mice. What am I?

Note to the teacher: Use with "My Riddle Book of Animals" on page 23.

Booklet Page

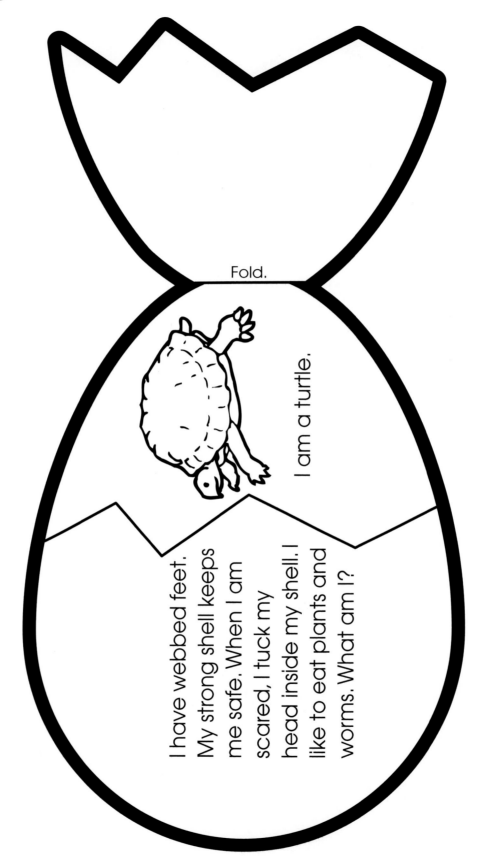

Fold.

I am a turtle.

I have webbed feet. My strong shell keeps me safe. When I am scared, I tuck my head inside my shell. I like to eat plants and worms. What am I?

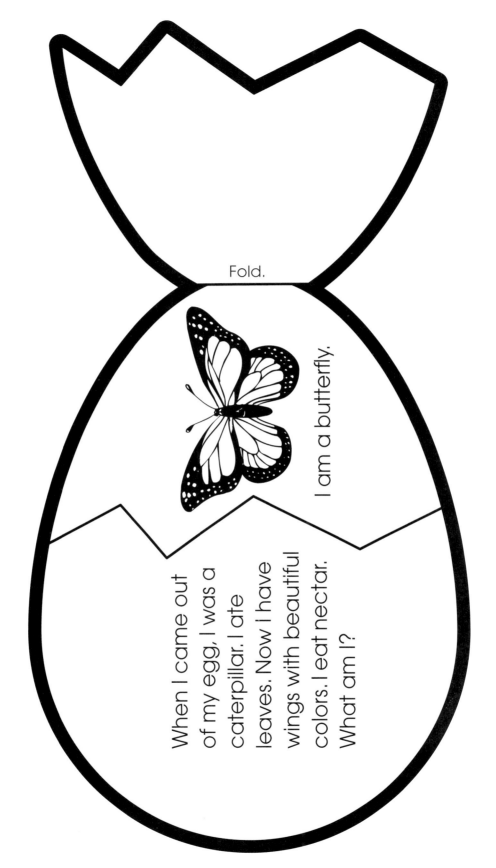

Fold.

I am a butterfly.

When I came out of my egg, I was a caterpillar. I ate leaves. Now I have wings with beautiful colors. I eat nectar. What am I?

©2000 The Education Center, Inc. • *I Can Make It! I Can Read It!* • *Spring* • TEC3507

Note to the teacher: Use with "My Riddle Book of Animals" on page 23.

27

Booklet Page

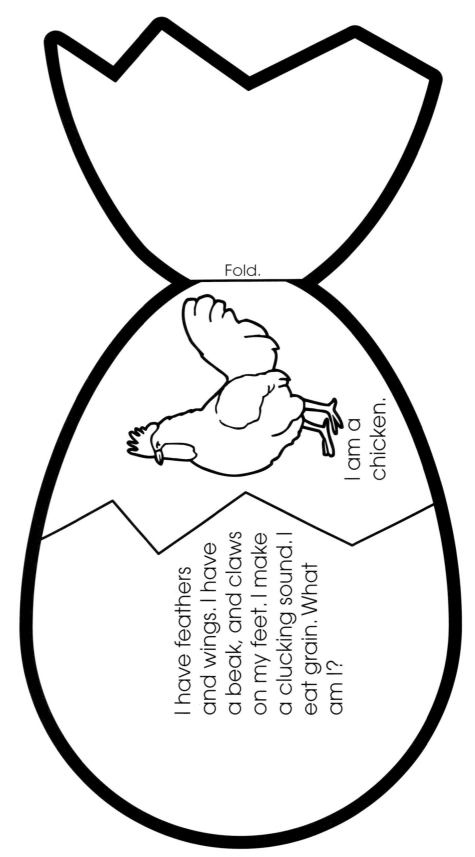

Fold.

I am a chicken.

I have feathers and wings. I have a beak, and claws on my feet. I make a clucking sound. I eat grain. What am I?

Note to the teacher: Use with "My Riddle Book of Animals" on page 23.

BUSY BEES

Young readers will find reading this repetitive booklet to be a "bee-utiful" experience! Give each student a copy of pages 30–32. Have each student color her cover and booklet page 6. (Remind students to color lightly over the text so the page can be read.) Then instruct the student to cut out her cover and booklet pages. Next, direct her to stack her booklet pages in numerical order. Have her fold the cover where indicated and place her booklet pages inside. Staple the pages together at the top. Next, read a completed booklet with students. Provide time for students to practice reading their booklets with one another. Then encourage students to take their booklets home to share with family members. Parents are sure to buzz with excitement over this charming booklet!

CREATIVE DECORATING OPTIONS

- Press fingertips on a black ink pad. Then make fingerprint bees on the cover. Add antennae, wings, and black stripes to the fingerprint bees with a fine-point marker.
- On the cover, outline the beehive with puffy paint.

Extend this booklet activity by inviting a beekeeper to visit the classroom to explain her job.

Busy Bees

Beatrice
Name

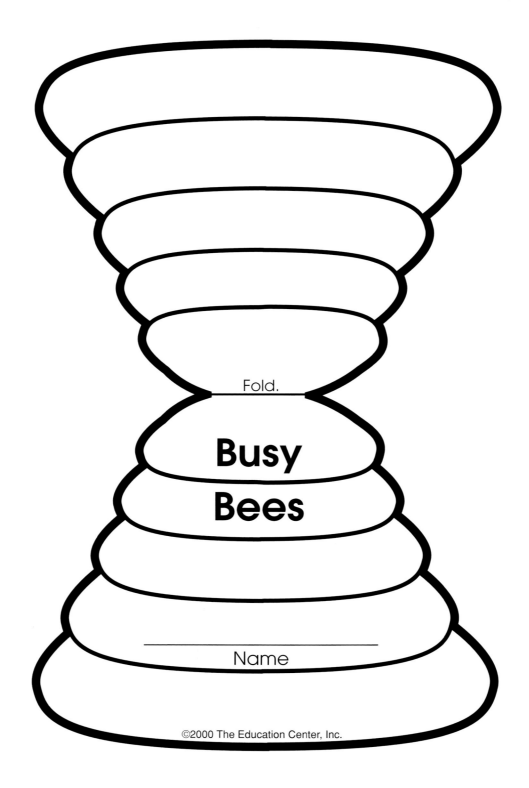

Fold.

Busy

Bees

_____
Name

©2000 The Education Center, Inc. • *I Can Make It! I Can Read It!* • *Spring* • TEC3507

30 Note to the teacher: Use with "Busy Bees" on page 29.

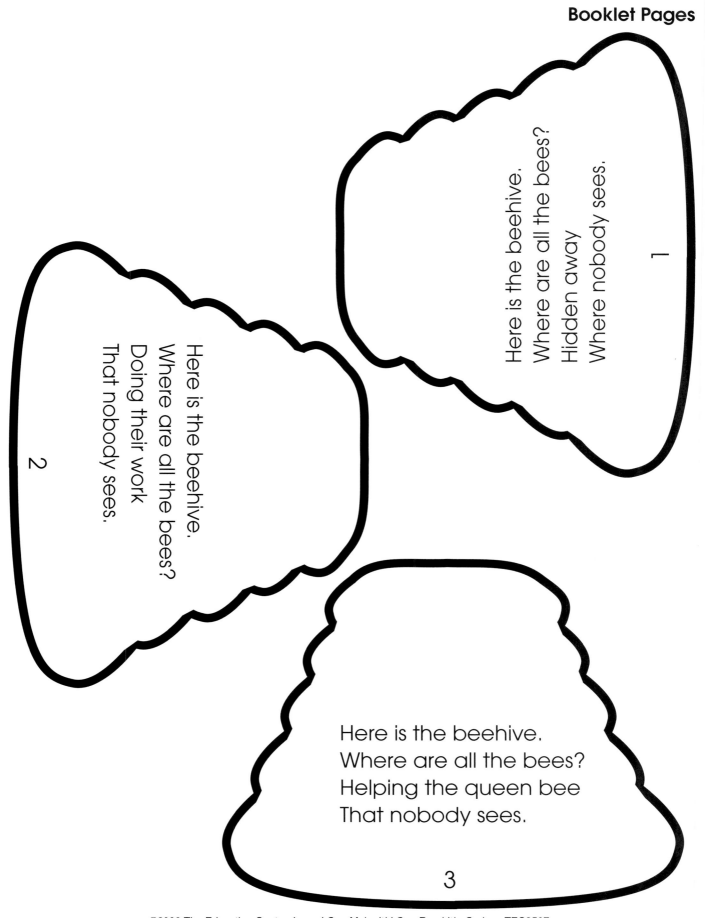

Here is the beehive.
Where are all the bees?
Hidden away
Where nobody sees.

1

Here is the beehive.
Where are all the bees?
Doing their work
That nobody sees.

2

Here is the beehive.
Where are all the bees?
Helping the queen bee
That nobody sees.

3

Note to the teacher: Use with "Busy Bees" on page 29.

Booklet Pages

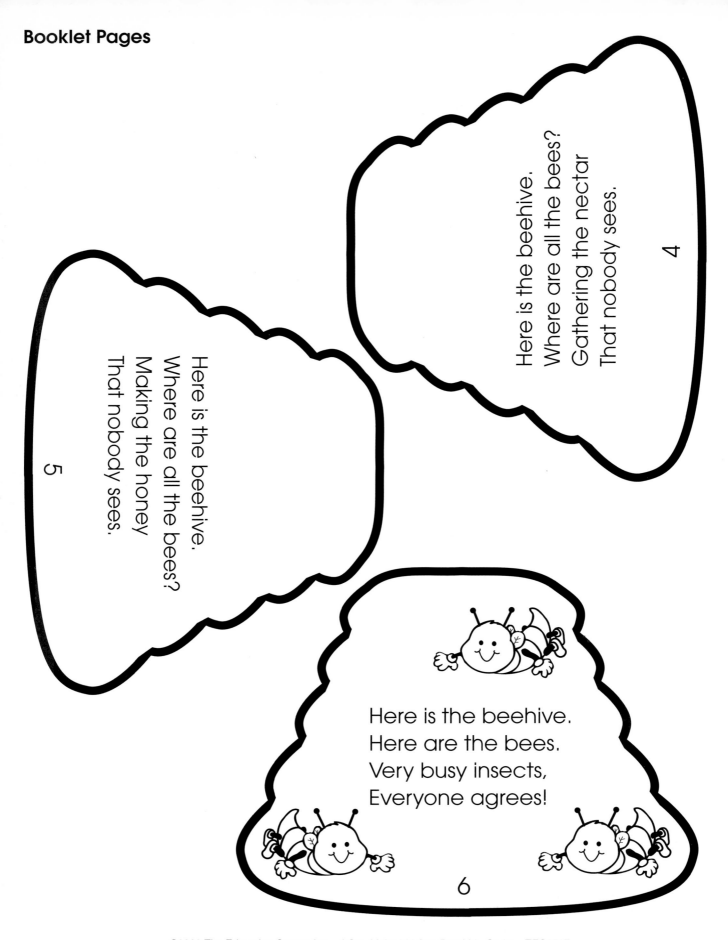

Here is the beehive.
Where are all the bees?
Gathering the nectar
That nobody sees.

4

Here is the beehive.
Where are all the bees?
Making the honey
That nobody sees.

5

Here is the beehive.
Here are the bees.
Very busy insects,
Everyone agrees!

6

KEEP AN EYE OUT FOR ANTS!

Use this informative booklet to stir up interest in one of nature's most amazing creatures—the ant! Give each student a copy of pages 34–38. Have the student color and cut out his booklet cover, pages, backing, and patterns. Next, instruct him to fold back the flaps of the shoe, sugar, grass, popcorn, and leaf; then have him glue them to the appropriate pages. Allow time for the glue to dry. Then direct him to stack his pages in numerical order, placing the cover on top. Staple the pages to the backing where indicated. Read a completed booklet with students, demonstrating how to lift the flaps to find the ants. Encourage each student to practice reading his booklet with a partner before taking it home to read to family members. Parents will be pleased to have these ants in their homes!

CREATIVE DECORATING OPTIONS

- On the backing, glue pipe cleaners to represent antennae.
- Glue colorful yarn around the edge of the cover.

To extend this booklet activity and see the world through the eyes of ants, read aloud Chris Van Allsburg's *Two Bad Ants* (Houghton Mifflin Company, 1988).

Keep an Eye Out for
Ants!

Phillip
Name

1

It can be good to have ants around. Ants eat a lot of bugs. But ants can be pests, too. Some ants have a sting that hurts! So watch where you step! Take a look. Can you find the ants?

5

Booklet Cover and Page

Cover

Keep an Eye Out for

Ants!

_____

Name

Page

Ants are all around us! Ants can be found on the ground, in a tree, or in your shoe. Take a look. Do you see any ants?

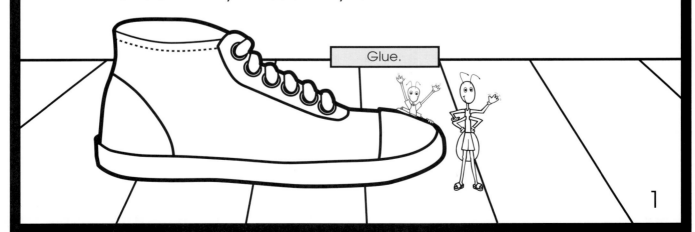

Glue.

1

Note to the teacher: Use with "Keep an Eye Out for Ants!" on page 33.

Ants live in nests. Some ants make their nests in the ground. These nests can be as big as a tennis court. Ten million ants can live in that big nest! Take a look. Can you find the ants?

Glue.

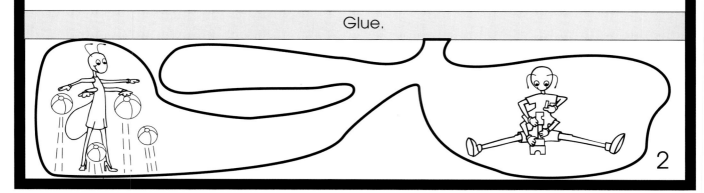

2

A nest can have one or more queen ants. The queen's job is to lay eggs.
A nest has lots of worker ants. Worker ants build the nest and look for food. Take a look. Can you find the ants?

Glue.

3

Note to the teacher: Use with "Keep an Eye Out for Ants!" on page 33.

An ant has two antennae on the front of its head. The ant smells, touches, tastes, and hears with its antennae. It uses its antennae to find food. Take a look. Can you find the ants?

Glue.

4

It can be good to have ants around. Ants eat a lot of bugs. But ants can be pests, too. Some ants have a sting that hurts! So watch where you step! Take a look. Can you find the ants?

Glue.

5

Note to the teacher: Use with "Keep an Eye Out for Ants!" on page 33.

Staple the booklet pages here.

©2000 The Education Center, Inc. • *I Can Make It! I Can Read It!* • *Spring* • TEC3507

Booklet Patterns

Shoe

Page 1

Popcorn

Page 4

Grass

Page 2

Sugar

Page 3

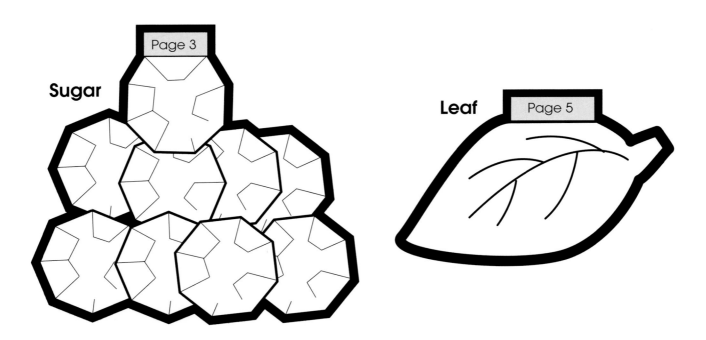

Leaf

Page 5

Note to the teacher: Use with "Keep an Eye Out for Ants!" on page 33.

THE BACKYARD BUNNY

Hop into learning with this warm and fuzzy informational booklet. Provide each student with a tagboard copy of page 40 and a copy of pages 41–42. Give each student a large white pom-pom. Have the student color and then cut out the tagboard backing. Direct him to glue the pom-pom tail to the backing. Have him color his cover. Direct him to cut out the cover and booklet pages. Instruct him to sequence the cover and booklet pages. Then have him staple them to the backing where indicated. When the booklets are finished, read one aloud. Invite student pairs to practice reading their booklets. Encourage your students to hop home and share their books with family members. Remind them to be on the lookout for backyard bunnies this spring!

CREATIVE DECORATING OPTIONS

• Glue Easter grass to the nest of the booklet backing.
• After the booklet pages are stapled in place, glue cotton fur to the bunny.

> To extend this activity, take your students to a nearby park or other natural area to look for bunnies and other spring babies.

The Backyard Bunny

Buddy
Name

Booklet Backing

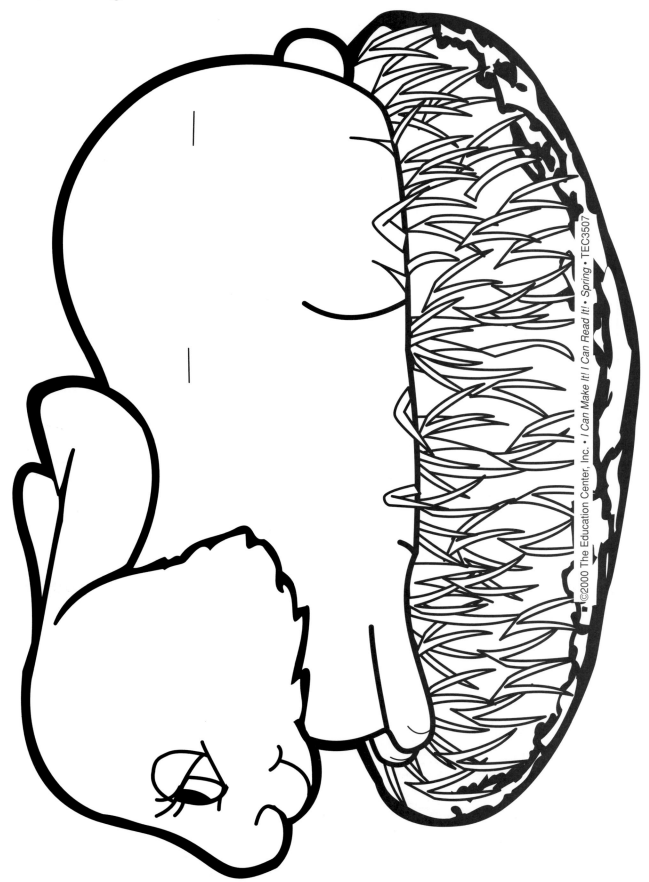

Note to the teacher: Use with "The Backyard Bunny" on page 39.

The Backyard Bunny

_____

Name

©2000 The Education Center, Inc.

The backyard bunny lives under the little red barn behind our house.

1

It is springtime and she is about to have babies.

2

She sleeps in the shade and nibbles the crisp, green grass.

3

Sometimes she eats the flowers that grow in our garden.

4

She digs a hole in the damp earth and lines it with dry grass and soft fur.

5

Note to the teacher: Use with "The Backyard Bunny" on page 39.

Booklet Pages

As she builds her nest, she keeps a close eye on the neighbor's cat.

6

When her babies are born, they are tiny and pink.

7

She snuggles on top of them to keep them warm.

8

Soon the babies grow fur. Their ears grow longer.

9

They hop out of the nest under the barn and sniff at the grass.

10

Now we have a whole family of backyard bunnies!

11

©2000 The Education Center, Inc. • *I Can Make It! I Can Read It!* • *Spring* • TEC3507

Note to the teacher: Use with "The Backyard Bunny" on page 39.

PETUNIA THE PIG

Youngsters will go hog-wild over this repetitive booklet! Give each student a copy of pages 44–48. Have the student cut out his cover and booklet pages along the bold outer lines. Instruct him to stack his pages in numerical order, placing the cover on top. Staple the booklets at the left. Then read a booklet with students. Direct the student to color in the missing parts (rabbit ears on page 3; rabbit ears and horse tail on page 5; and rabbit ears, horse tail, and cow coat on page 7). Next, invite him to color the booklet illustrations. When the booklets are finished, read one aloud with students. Then encourage each student to practice reading his booklet with a partner before taking it home to read to family members.

CREATIVE DECORATING OPTIONS

- Glue felt rabbit ears on the pig.
- Glue a tail made of brown yarn on the pig.

Extend this booklet activity by discovering the humorous outcome of a pig invasion! Read aloud *Pigs Aplenty, Pigs Galore!* by David McPhail (Puffin Books, 1997).

Booklet Cover and Page

Cover

Petunia the Pig

_____
Name

Page

Petunia the pig was a happy pig. Petunia liked the way she looked.

1

Note to the teacher: Use with "Petunia the Pig" on page 43.

One day Petunia went for a walk. While walking, she met a rabbit. "You look funny!" said the rabbit. "You need ears like mine."

2

Petunia was not so happy. So she made herself some new ears and put them on.

3

Note to the teacher: Use with "Petunia the Pig" on page 43.

Then she met a horse. "You look funny!" said the horse. "You need a tail like mine."

4

Petunia was not so happy. So she made herself a new tail and put it on.

5

Then she met a cow. "You look funny!" said the cow. "You need a coat like mine."

6

Petunia was not so happy. So she made herself a new coat and put it on.

7

Note to the teacher: Use with "Petunia the Pig" on page 43.

Then she met a pig friend. "You look funny!" said the pig friend. "You are a funny pig."

8

So Petunia took off her long ears, her long tail, and her spotted coat. She liked the way she looked. Now Petunia was a happy pig!

9

ONE FINE SPRING DAY

This rhyming barnyard booklet will have youngsters crowing about reading! Give each student a copy of pages 51 and 52 and a red construction paper copy of page 50. Have the student color her illustrations. Then instruct her to cut out the booklet backing, cover, pages, and illustrations along the bold outer lines. Have her cut the barn door along the dotted lines. Direct her to stack her booklet pages in numerical order, place the cover on top, and then staple the pages to the backing where indicated. Next, have her stack her illustrations in numerical order, place them behind the barn door, and staple them to the left side of the door as shown. Read a completed booklet with students, demonstrating how to turn an illustration page to match a text page. Then provide time for each student to practice reading her booklet with a buddy. Once the student has gained proficiency reading her booklet, have her take her booklet home to read to family members. Youngsters will certainly be in the "moo-d" to read!

CREATIVE DECORATING OPTIONS

- Glue raffia, straw, or yarn at the hayloft door.
- Use scraps of construction paper to make a farmer and glue him next to the barn door.

Extend this booklet activity by reading aloud *New Baby Calf* by Edith N. Chase (Scholastic Paperbacks, 1991).

One Fine Spring Day

by _____
Shelly

's barn

Booklet Backing

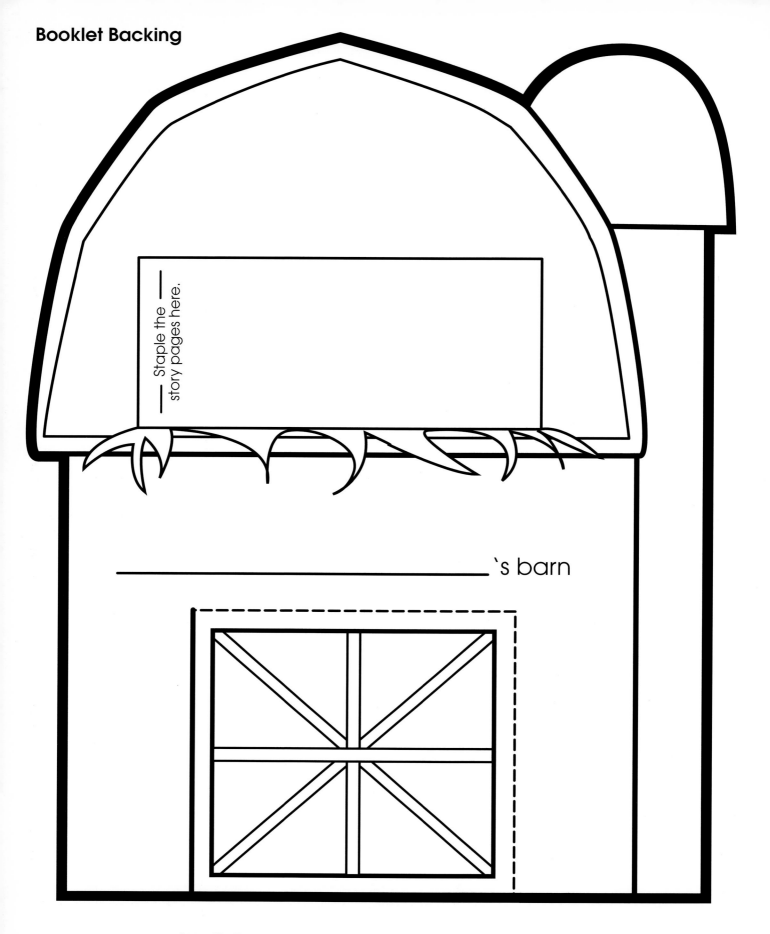

— Staple the — story pages here.

_____ 's barn

Cover

One Fine Spring Day

by _____

©2000 The Education Center, Inc.

1

When he went to the barn one fine spring day,
Farmer Greene carried corn and oats and hay.
A moment later, he ran back out.
He whooped and hollered and gave a shout.

2

"Come quick!" said the farmer. "A yellow chick.
The hen has a chick. Come quick! Come quick!"

3

"Look now!" said the farmer. "Look at the cow.
There's a calf with the cow. Look now! Look now!"

4

"Call the vet!" said the farmer. "A pink piglet!
The sow has a piglet. Call the vet. Call the vet!"

5

"It's true!" said the farmer. "See the ewe?
There's a lamb with the ewe. It's true! It's true!"

6

He went to his house that fine spring day,
To tell his wife and see what she'd say.
A moment later, he ran back out.
He whooped and hollered and gave a shout.

7

"Oh, joy!" said the farmer. "A baby boy!
My wife has a baby. Oh, joy! Oh, joy!"

Note to the teacher: Use with "One Fine Spring Day" on page 49.

Booklet Illustrations

Note to the teacher: Use with "One Fine Spring Day" on page 49.

BENNY PLANTS A SURPRISE!

Cultivate reading skills with this repetitive booklet! Give each student a copy of pages 54–56. Have the student color and cut out the booklet cover, pages, and pattern. (Remind students to color lightly over the text so the story can still be read.) Then direct the student to cut the slit on booklet page 5. Instruct him to stack his pages in numerical order and place the cover on top. Staple the pages on the left-hand side of the booklet. Next, read a completed booklet with students. Ask the class what kind of seeds Benny planted. Then have each student fill in the answer on his carrot and insert it through the slit. Provide time for students to practice reading their booklets with one another. Encourage each student to take his booklet home to read to family members. This bunny tale will help young readers flourish!

CREATIVE DECORATING OPTIONS
- Glue seeds to the cover.
- On each page, illustrate what Benny Bunny does.

Extend this booklet activity by reading aloud *The Carrot Seed* by Ruth Krauss (HarperTrophy, 1989), a story about a little boy who truly believes his carrot seeds will grow.

ed carrot seeds.

Benny Plants a Surprise!

Carlos
Name

The small bushy green plants grow and grow. Benny wants to find out what kind of seeds he planted. He pulls and pulls on a plant. Up pops a big, orange carrot!

5

Booklet Page and Cover

Page

Benny Bunny helps Mama Bunny plant a garden. Mama Bunny gives Benny some seeds to plant.

"What kind of seeds are these?" Benny asks.

"Wait and see," Mama says.

1

Cover

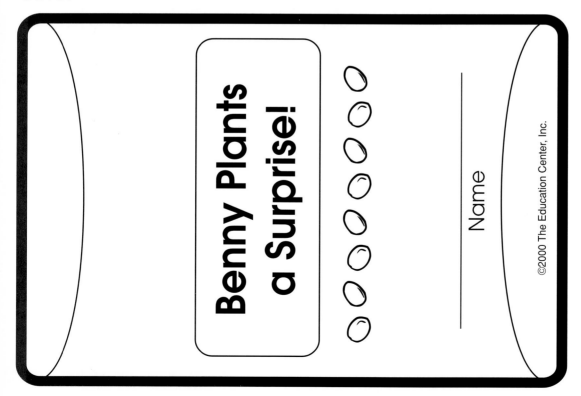

Benny Plants a Surprise!

Name _____

©2000 The Education Center, Inc. • *I Can Make It! I Can Read It!* • *Spring* • TEC3507

54   **Note to the teacher:** Use with "Benny Plants a Surprise!" on page 53.

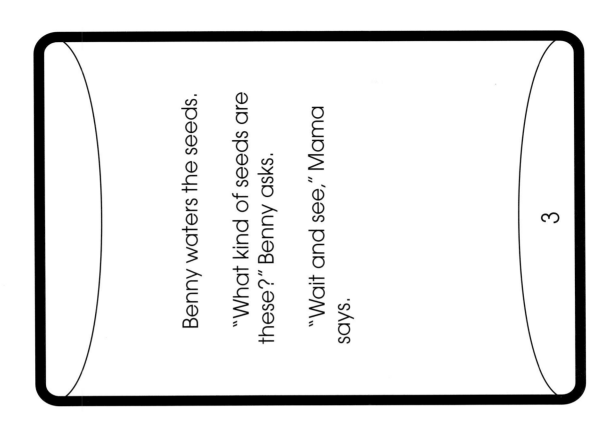

Benny waters the seeds.

"What kind of seeds are these?" Benny asks.

"Wait and see," Mama says.

3

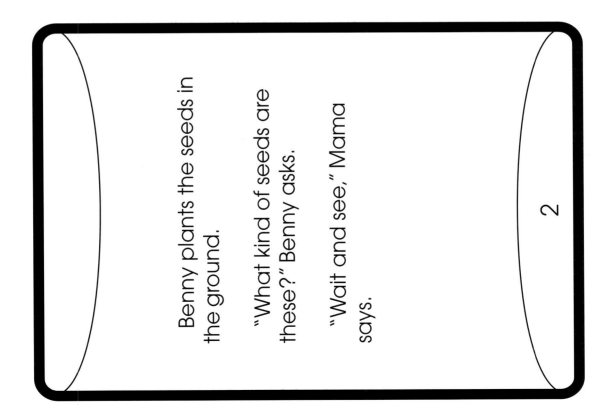

Benny plants the seeds in the ground.

"What kind of seeds are these?" Benny asks.

"Wait and see," Mama says.

2

Booklet Pages and Pattern

The small bushy green plants grow and grow. Benny wants to find out what kind of seeds he planted. He pulls and pulls on a plant. Up pops a big, orange carrot!

5

Carrot

Benny planted _____ seeds.

The sun shines on the garden. Benny sees something pushing up through the ground.

"What kind of plants are these?" Benny asks.

"Wait and see," Mama says.

4

Note to the teacher: Use with "Benny Plants a Surprise!" on page 53.

DRIP! DROP! DRIP!

Welcome spring with this splashy mobile-style booklet! Give each student a copy of pages 58–60. Provide a hole puncher, scissors, crayons, rulers, and blue yarn. Have each student measure and then cut ten ten-inch lengths of yarn. Direct the student to color her cover, booklet pages, and flower patterns, and then cut them out. Instruct her to hole-punch each page and the flower patterns where indicated. Then have her use the yarn to tie the booklet pages, cover, and flower patterns together as shown. When the booklets are finished, read one aloud. Invite students to practice reading their booklets with other class members. Encourage your students to read their books with family members and then hang them up to bring sunny smiles to those rainy spring days!

CREATIVE DECORATING OPTION

- Dab glue on the cover and booklet pages, and then sprinkle with blue glitter.

Extend this booklet by reciting the text of "Drip! Drop! Drip!" as you lead students in a movement activity.

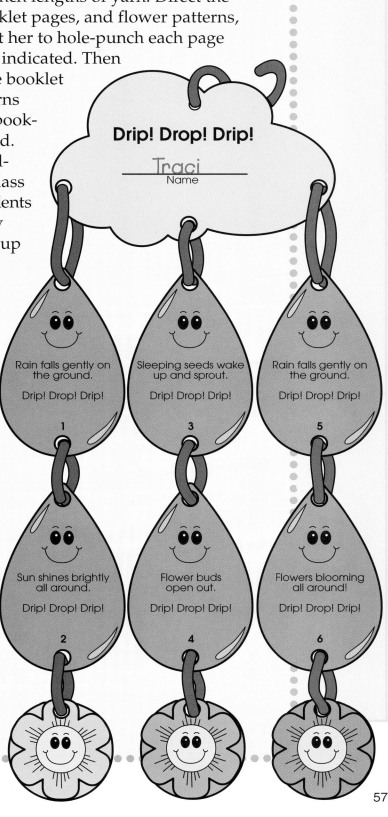

Drip! Drop! Drip!

Traci
Name

Rain falls gently on the ground.
Drip! Drop! Drip!
1

Sleeping seeds wake up and sprout.
Drip! Drop! Drip!
3

Rain falls gently on the ground.
Drip! Drop! Drip!
5

Sun shines brightly all around.
Drip! Drop! Drip!
2

Flower buds open out.
Drip! Drop! Drip!
4

Flowers blooming all around!
Drip! Drop! Drip!
6

Booklet Cover and Flower Patterns

Cover

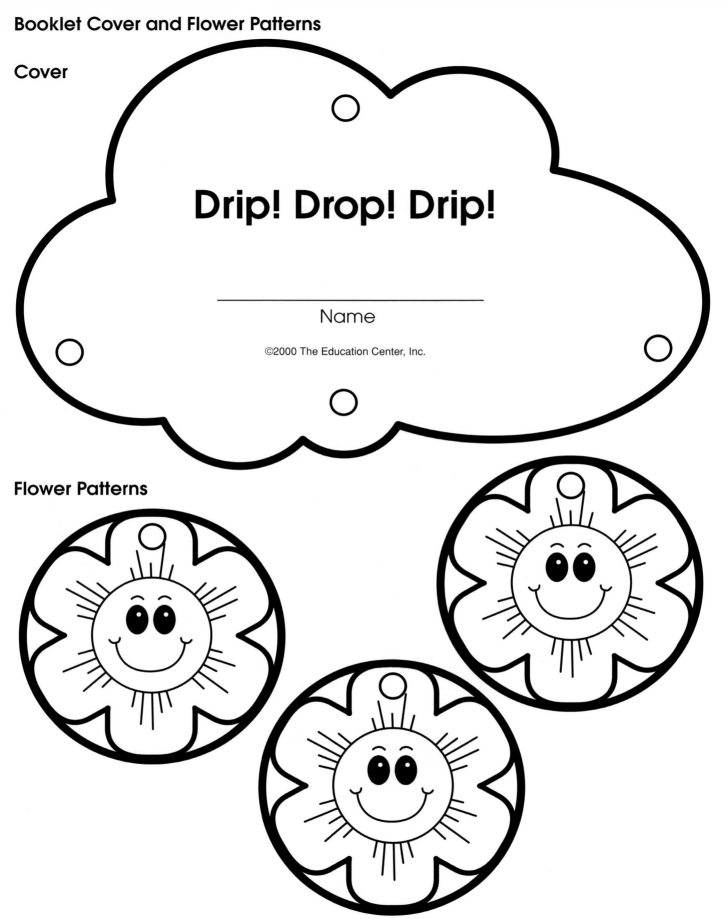

Drip! Drop! Drip!

_____
Name

Flower Patterns

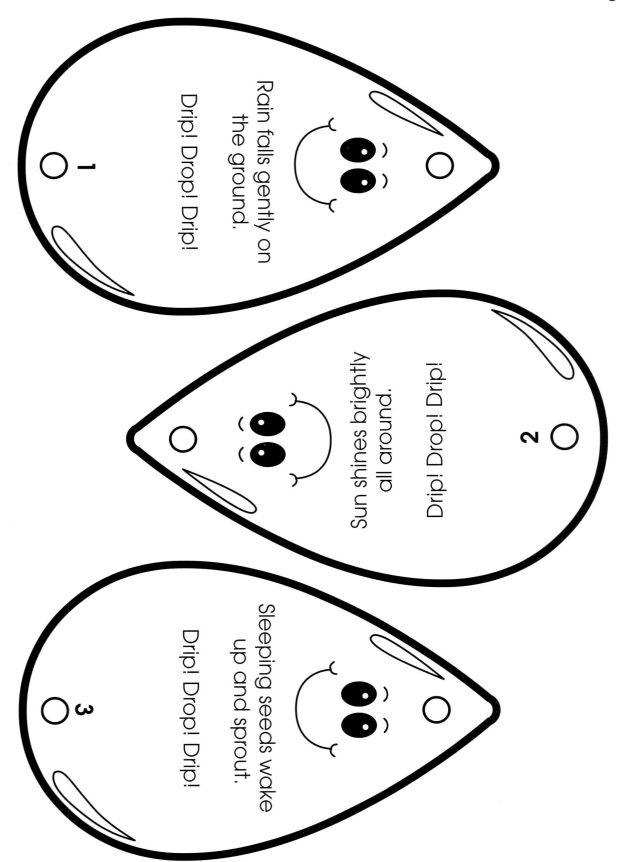

Drip! Drop! Drip!

Rain falls gently on the ground.

1

Drip! Drop! Drip!

Sun shines brightly all around.

2

Sleeping seeds wake up and sprout.

Drip! Drop! Drip!

3

Booklet Pages

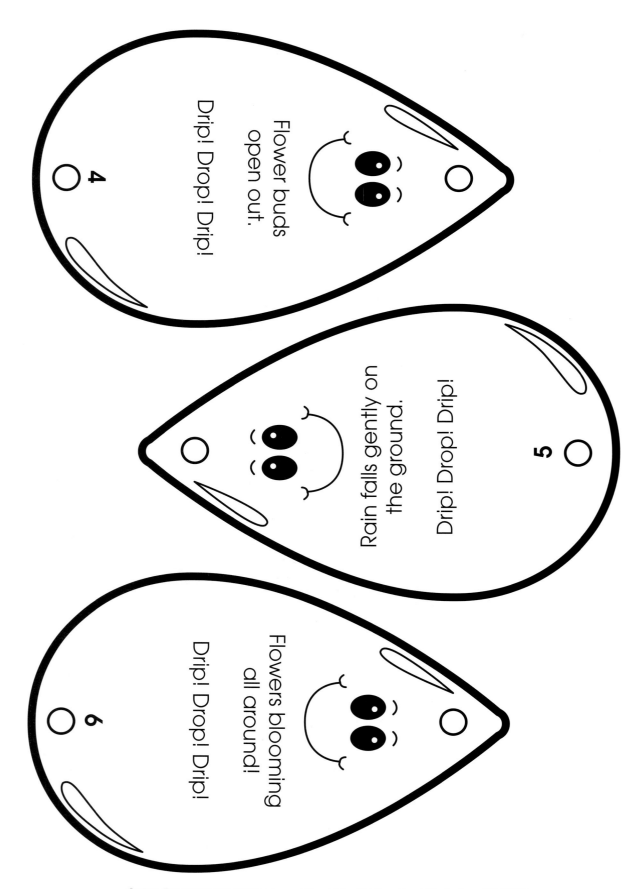

4

Drip! Drop! Drip!

Flower buds
open out.

5

Rain falls gently on
the ground.

Drip! Drop! Drip!

6

Flowers blooming
all around!

Drip! Drop! Drip!

RAINBOW GARDEN

Visit a colorful garden and watch reader confidence grow with this rainbow booklet! Give each student a copy of pages 62–66. Read the booklet pages with students. Then have each student color his booklet backing and patterns according to the corresponding text. Instruct him to cut out the backing, patterns, cover, and pages along the bold outer lines. Next, have him arrange the flowers, bird, and birdhouse on the backing to match the text and then glue them into position. Direct the student to arrange his booklet pages in numerical order, placing the cover on top. Place the booklet pages at the bottom of the backing and staple them where indicated. Then read a completed booklet with students. Provide time for each student to practice reading his booklet with a buddy. Encourage students to take their booklets home to read to family members and friends. Parents will be delighted to see reading skills blooming!

CREATIVE DECORATING OPTIONS

- Use watercolors to paint the backing and patterns.
- Mount the booklet on a sheet of 9" x 12" construction paper. Then glue rainbow-colored yarn around the border.

To extend this booklet activity, show students how bulbs, seeds, and seedlings grow into a rainbow of blooms. Read to students *Planting a Rainbow* by Lois Ehlert (Harcourt Brace & Company, 1992).

Red tulips grow by the garden wall.

2

Booklet Cover and Pages

Cover

Rainbow Garden

_____
Name

Pages

My backyard is a rainbow of colors.

1

Red tulips grow by the garden wall.

2

Note to the teacher: Use with "Rainbow Garden" on page 61.

On the garden wall is an orange birdhouse. Inside the birdhouse is a nest of baby birds.

3

Near the birdhouse, a yellow sunflower is growing tall. Birds come and eat sunflower seeds.

4

Near the garden is green grass. The grass is home for many bugs. Some of the bugs are green, too!

5

Note to the teacher: Use with "Rainbow Garden" on page 61.

In the spring, a bluebird sits on the garden wall. She catches bugs to feed her babies.

6

Purple balloon flowers grow wild on the ground.

7

Red, orange, yellow, green, blue, and purple. My backyard is a rainbow of colors!

8

Staple the booklet pages here.

Note to the teacher: Use with "Rainbow Garden" on page 61.

Booklet Patterns

Sunflower

Bluebird

Birdhouse

Balloon Flowers

Tulips

Note to the teacher: Use with "Rainbow Garden" on page 61.

TAKING CARE OF OUR EARTH

Strengthen reading skills and teach conservation with this Earth Day booklet. Give each student a copy of pages 69 and 70 and a white construction paper copy of page 68. Have the student color her backing and then cut it and the booklet pages out along the bold outer lines. Next, direct the student to glue the cloud with the gray box to its matching cloud as shown. Then have her fold the pages on the thin lines so the text is not showing. On the backing, have her apply glue to the gray boxes where indicated. Instruct her to place a cloud on each of the gray boxes (see the illustration). When the glue has dried, read a booklet with students. Then provide time for students to practice reading their booklets with one another. Encourage students to take their booklets home to read to family members and friends.

CREATIVE DECORATING OPTIONS

- Paint the backing with watercolors.
- Glue cotton balls to the clouds.

Extend this booklet activity by reminding students that we cannot take our world for granted. Read aloud *The Wump World* by Bill Peet (Houghton Mifflin Company, 1991).

Save Trees
What can you do to use fewer trees?

Use as few things made of paper as you can. Here are three ways you can help save trees.

1. Clean up spills with a sponge, not with a paper towel.
2. Use both sides of a sheet of paper.
3. Recycle your newspapers.

Taking Care of Our
Earth

2. Use both sides of a sheet of paper.
3. Recycle your newspapers.

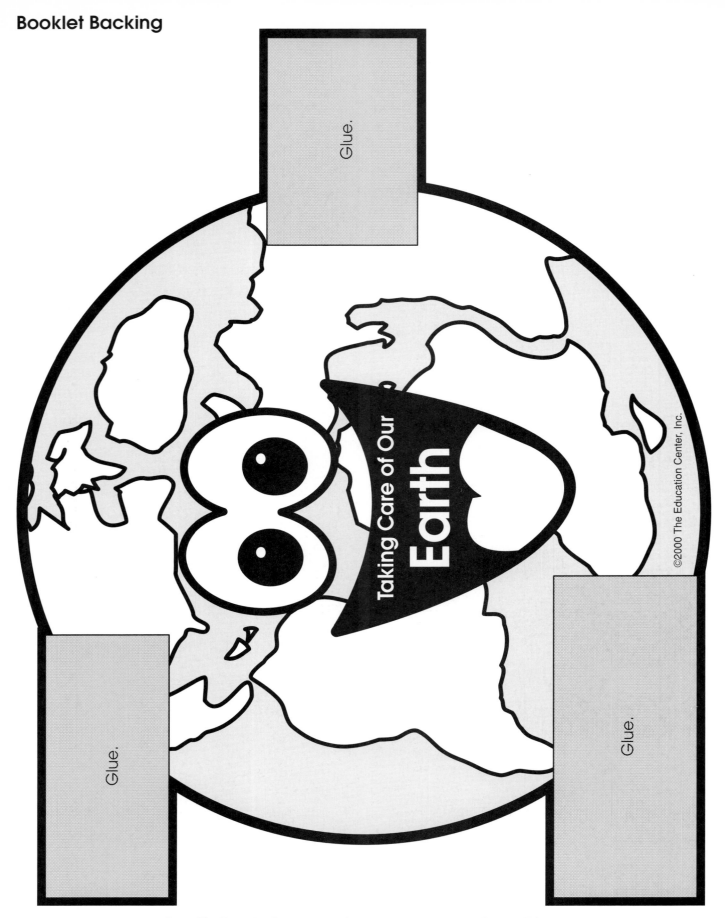

Glue.

Glue.

Glue.

Taking Care of Our Earth

©2000 The Education Center, Inc.

©2000 The Education Center, Inc. • *I Can Make It! I Can Read It!* • *Spring* • TEC3507

68   **Note to the teacher:** Use with "Taking Care of Our Earth" on page 67.

Save Water

What can you do to use less water?

Use as little water as possible. Here are three ways you can help save water.

1. Turn the water off while brushing your teeth.
2. When you turn off the water at a sink, make sure the water does not drip.
3. When you take a bath, do not fill the tub with more water than you need.

Use as few things made of paper as you can. Here are three ways you can help save trees.

1. Clean up spills with a sponge, not with a paper towel.
2. Use both sides of a sheet of paper.
3. Recycle your newspapers.

Note to the teacher: Use with "Taking Care of Our Earth" on page 67.

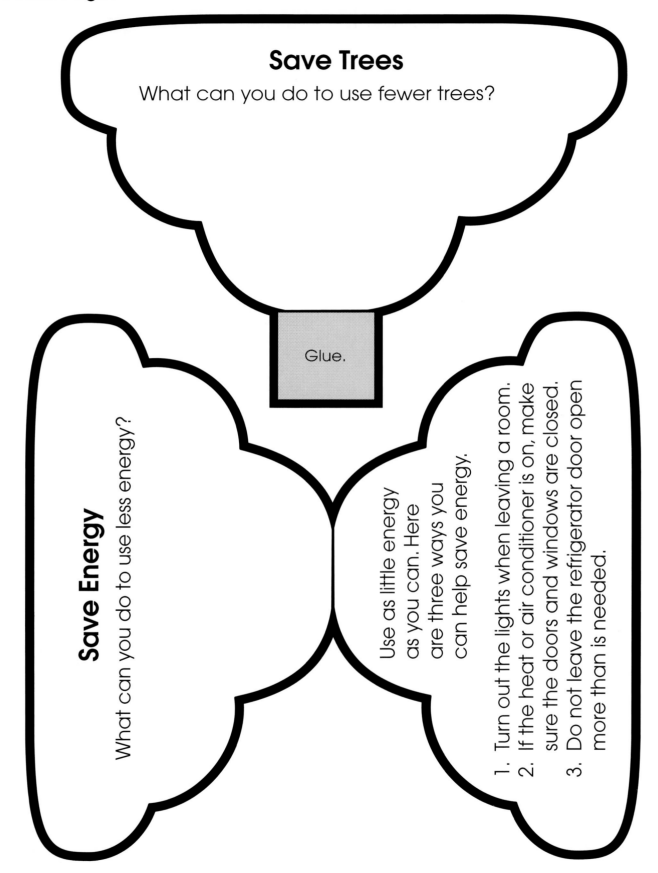

Save Trees

What can you do to use fewer trees?

Glue.

Save Energy

What can you do to use less energy?

Use as little energy as you can. Here are three ways you can help save energy.

1. Turn out the lights when leaving a room.
2. If the heat or air conditioner is on, make sure the doors and windows are closed.
3. Do not leave the refrigerator door open more than is needed.

THE POND WHERE TIMOTHY LIVES

This repetitive booklet is sure to make a big splash with your youngsters! Give each student a copy of pages 72–74. Have her color and cut out her cover and booklet pages. Next, instruct her to stack her pages in numerical order, placing the cover on top. Staple each booklet at the top. Then read a completed booklet with students. Provide time for each student to practice reading her booklet with a partner. Encourage students to take their booklets home to read to family members and friends. Reading about pond life is bound to "wet" students' appetites for more reading!

CREATIVE DECORATING OPTIONS

- Paint the pond with watercolors to create a watery effect.
- Using crayons or fine-point markers, draw pond plants and insects on the cover.

Extend this booklet activity by reading aloud *Around the Pond: Who's Been Here?* by Lindsay Barrett George (Greenwillow Books, 1996).

This is the pond where Timothy lives.

1

Booklet Cover and Page

Cover

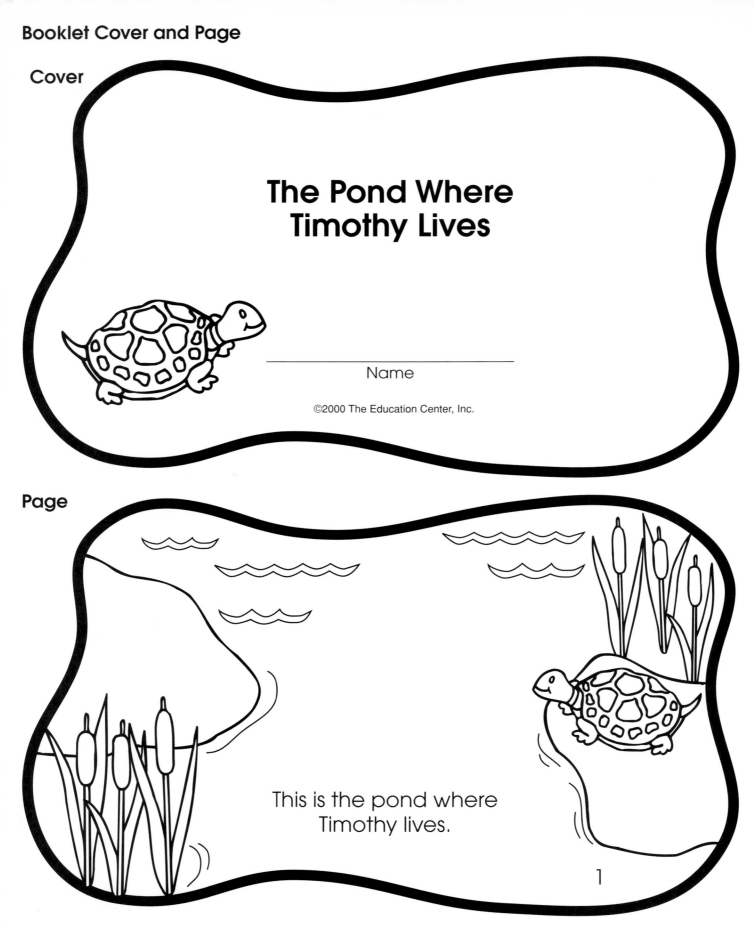

The Pond Where Timothy Lives

_____
Name

Page

This is the pond where Timothy lives.

1

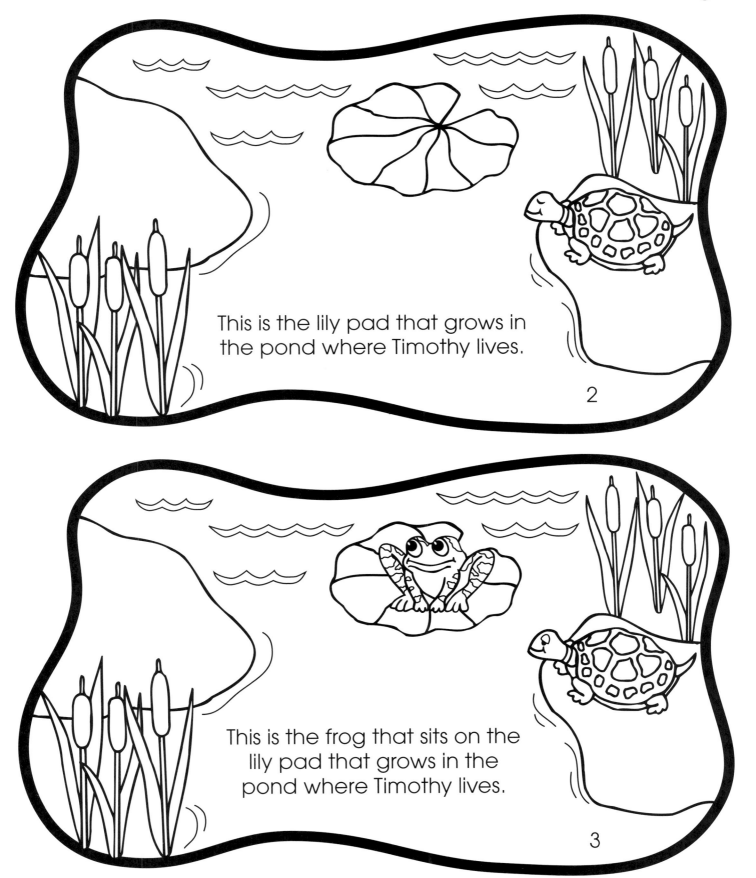

This is the lily pad that grows in the pond where Timothy lives.

2

This is the frog that sits on the lily pad that grows in the pond where Timothy lives.

3

Note to the teacher: Use with "The Pond Where Timothy Lives" on page 71.

Booklet Pages

This is the fish that swims under the frog that sits on the lily pad that grows in the pond where Timothy lives.

4

This is the boy who catches the fish that bumps the lily pad that flips the frog that makes a big splash in the pond where Timothy lives.

5

Note to the teacher: Use with "The Pond Where Timothy Lives" on page 71.

PLAY IT SAFE!

Watch your youngsters get pumped up about reading *and* bicycle safety with this informative booklet! Give each student a copy of pages 77–78, a white construction paper copy of page 76, and a brad. Have the student color her booklet backing and arm patterns. Then instruct her to cut out the backing, arms, and booklet pages. Direct her to hole-punch the two arms and the biker's shoulder where indicated. Have her insert the brad through the shoulder and arms as illustrated. Next, instruct her to stack the booklet pages in numerical order and place the cover on top. Then staple the booklet pages to the backing where indicated, being careful not to staple the arms. Read a completed booklet with students, rotating the arms to demonstrate the different arm signals. Then encourage students to take their booklets home to read to family members.

CREATIVE DECORATING OPTION

- Before attaching the booklet pages, color scenery in the background.

> To extend this booklet activity, read aloud Marc Brown's *D. W. Rides Again!* (Little, Brown and Company; 1996). Youngsters will delight in D. W.'s experience learning to ride her bicycle.

Play It Safe!

Shannon
Name

We use our left arms to let others know what we are going to do.

left turn   slow down or stop   right turn

Booklet Backing and Patterns

Arms

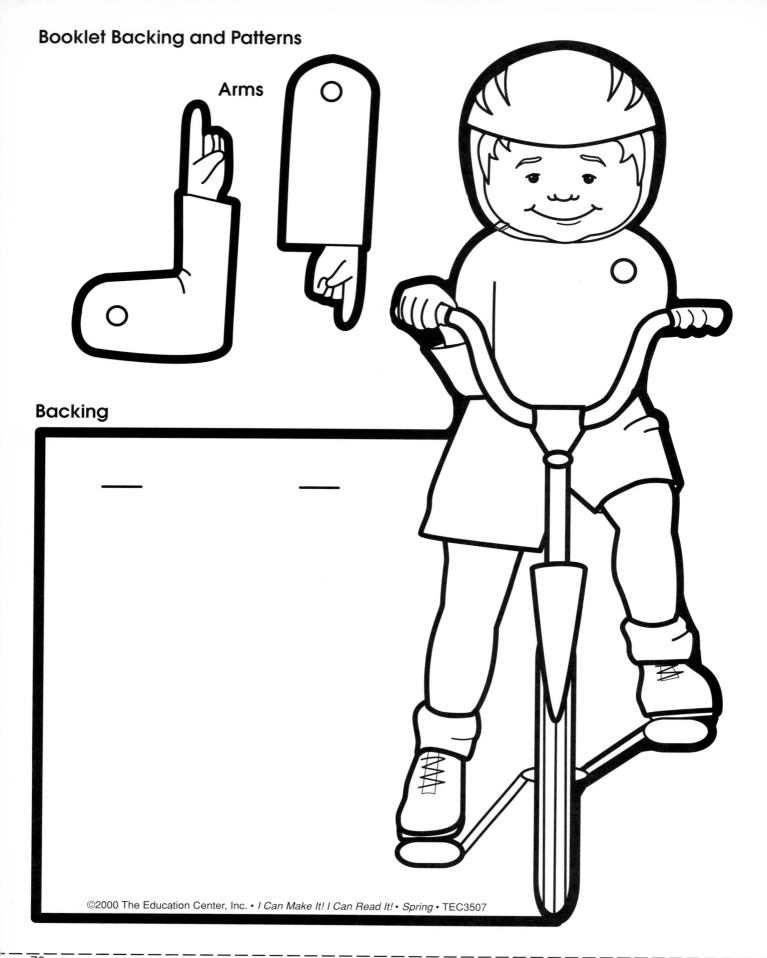

Backing

Note to the teacher: Use with "Play It Safe!" on page 75.

Cover **Pages**

Play It Safe!

_____

Name

My family and I go bike riding every Sunday.

We always wear our helmets.

1

We always watch for cars.

2

We stop and look both ways

at every intersection.

3

We use our left arms to let others know what we are going to do.

| left turn | slow down or stop | right turn |

4

We keep to the right side of the road.

5

We ride in a line with one rider behind the other.

6

We play it safe!

7

LET'S EAT STRAWBERRIES!

Sweeten your reading program with this appetizing strawberry booklet! Give each student a copy of pages 81–84 and a red construction paper copy of page 80. If desired, instruct the student to color the illustrations. Have her cut out the covers and booklet pages along the bold outer lines. Next, have her stack her pages in numerical order, placing the front cover on top and the back cover on the bottom. Staple the booklet at the top. Then read a completed booklet with students. Provide time for each student to practice reading with a buddy. Encourage students to take their booklets home to read to family members and friends. Parents will find this mouthwatering booklet irresistible!

CREATIVE DECORATING OPTIONS

- Make a template of the cover's strawberry cap. Trace the template onto a piece of green construction paper. Glue the resulting shape on the cover's strawberry cap.
- Glue wiggle eyes on the cover.

Extend this booklet activity by having students make peanut butter and strawberry jam sandwiches. Using a strawberry-shaped cookie cutter, direct students to cut out the sandwiches. Serve the sandwiches with milk for a "berry" delicious treat.

Let's Eat Strawberries!

Stacey
Name

Booklet Covers

Front Cover

Let's Eat Strawberries!

_____
Name

©2000 The Education Center, Inc.

Back Cover

Note to the teacher: Use with "Let's Eat Strawberries!" on page 79.

Everyone in my family likes to eat strawberries.

1

Grandpa eats big, sweet strawberries right after they have been picked and washed.

2

Note to the teacher: Use with "Let's Eat Strawberries!" on page 79.

Grandma likes strawberry shortcake with whipped cream.

3

Mom likes pancakes with strawberries on top.

4

Dad likes to eat big slices of strawberry pie.

5

My sister likes peanut butter and strawberry jam sandwiches.

6

Note to the teacher: Use with "Let's Eat Strawberries!" on page 79.

My brother loves to drink strawberry milkshakes.

7

I like to eat a big, cold strawberry ice-cream cone.

Ask my family, "What do you want to eat?"
"Let's eat strawberries!"

8

TAKE A LOOK INSIDE!

Bone up on the human body *and* boost reading skills with this fascinating booklet! Give each student a copy of pages 86–88. Have the student color and cut out her booklet pages and backing. Then instruct her to stack her booklet pages in numerical order and staple them to the backing where indicated. Next, read a completed booklet with students. Provide time for each student to practice reading her booklet with a partner. Then send the booklets home for students to read to family members and friends.

CREATIVE DECORATING OPTIONS

- Outline the bones with white glue or white puffy paint.
- Glue a photograph of the student on top of the head on the backing.

> To extend this booklet activity and teach youngsters more about the human body, read aloud *Me and My Body* by Rosie McCormick (Larousse Kingfisher Chambers, Inc.; 1998).

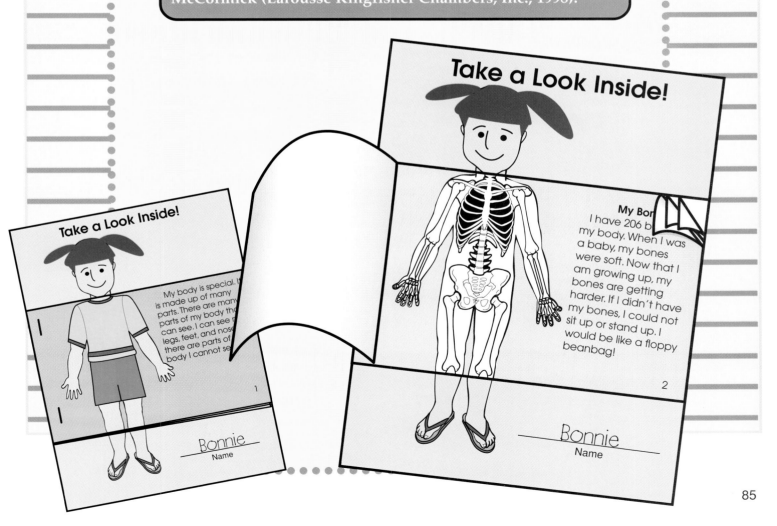

Take a Look Inside!

My body is special. It is made up of many parts. There are many parts of my body that I can see. I can see my legs, feet, and nose. But there are parts of my body I cannot see.

1

Bonnie
Name

Take a Look Inside!

My Bones
I have 206 bones in my body. When I was a baby, my bones were soft. Now that I am growing up, my bones are getting harder. If I didn't have my bones, I could not sit up or stand up. I would be like a floppy beanbag!

2

Bonnie
Name

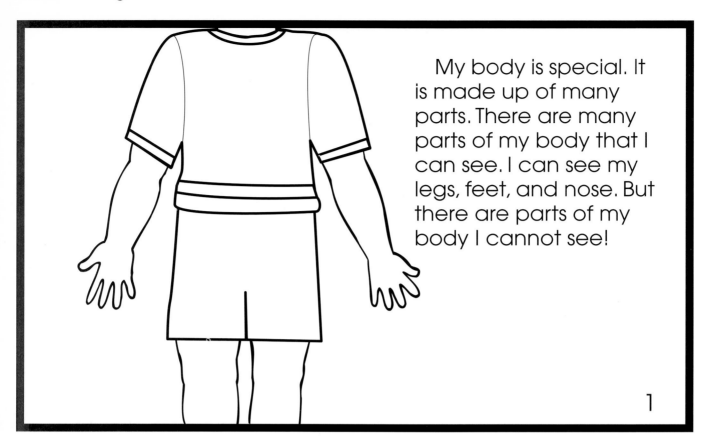

My body is special. It is made up of many parts. There are many parts of my body that I can see. I can see my legs, feet, and nose. But there are parts of my body I cannot see!

1

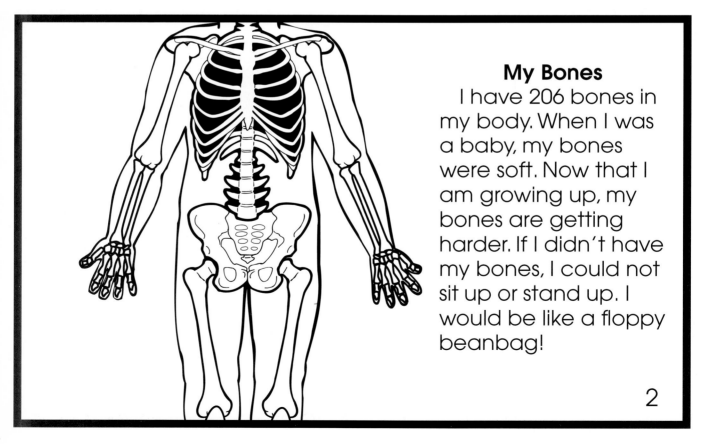

My Bones
I have 206 bones in my body. When I was a baby, my bones were soft. Now that I am growing up, my bones are getting harder. If I didn't have my bones, I could not sit up or stand up. I would be like a floppy beanbag!

2

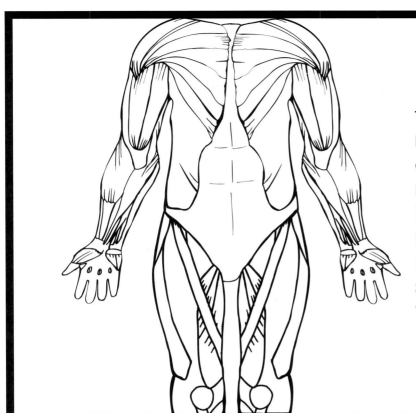

My Muscles

I have muscles all through my body. My muscles help me run and jump. My strongest muscles are in my back. My smallest muscle is in my ear. Some of my muscles work when I sit still. Some even work while I sleep!

3

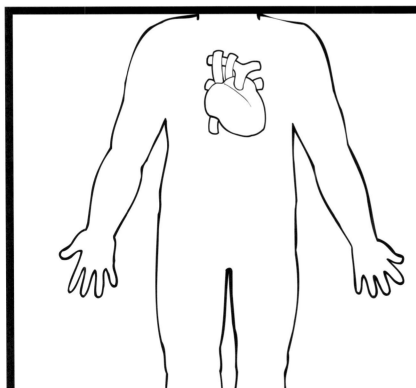

My Heart

My heart sends blood through my body. When I run, my heart beats fast. When I sit and read, my heart beats slower. My heart is strong. In an hour, my heart works hard enough to pick up a small car!

4

Note to the teacher: Use with "Take a Look Inside!" on page 85.

Take a Look Inside!

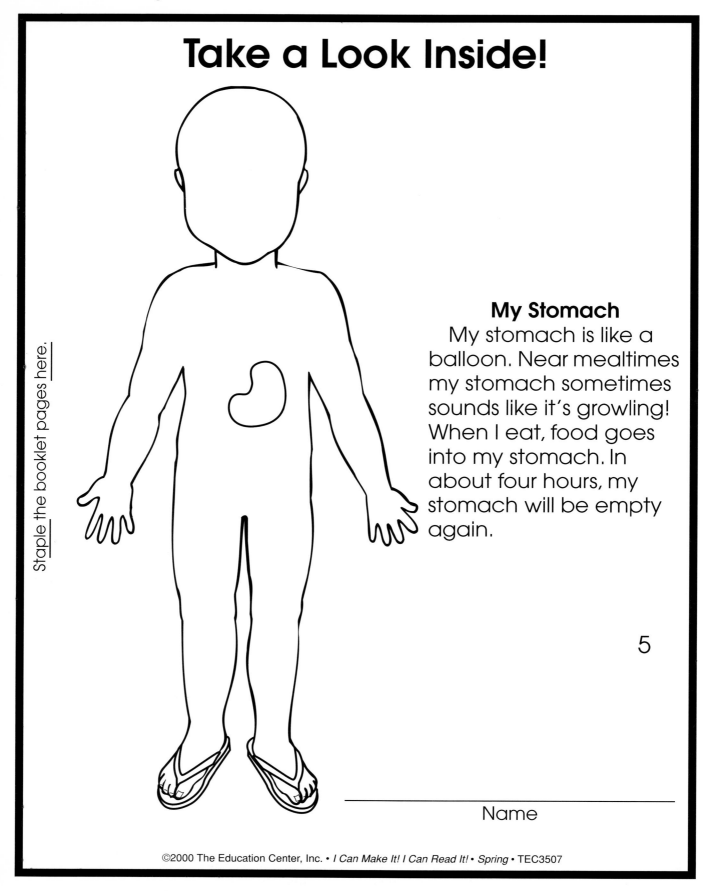

Staple the booklet pages here.

My Stomach

My stomach is like a balloon. Near mealtimes my stomach sometimes sounds like it's growling! When I eat, food goes into my stomach. In about four hours, my stomach will be empty again.

5

_____
Name

KEEPING HEALTHY

Challenge youngsters to keep a journal of the many ways they can keep healthy with this energizing booklet! Give each student a copy of pages 91 and 92 and a construction paper copy of page 90. Have each student cut out his booklet cover and pages along the bold outer lines. Next, help him cut a slit along the cover's dotted line. Invite him to color the illustrations on each booklet page. Then direct him to fold his cover on the thin line. Have the student stack his pages in numerical order and place them inside the cover. Staple the journal on the left-hand side. Read a completed journal with students and then demonstrate how to insert the lock into the journal. Next, provide time daily for each student to read and mark his journal pages appropriately. At the end of the week, encourage each student to read his journal with a friend. Then invite students to take their journals home to read to family members.

CREATIVE DECORATING OPTIONS

- Glue magazine pictures of examples of healthy practices, such as someone eating an apple, to the booklet cover.
- On the cover, glue a photograph of the student doing something healthy, such as washing his hands.

Extend this booklet activity by having students pantomime healthy activities, such as brushing teeth. Have classmates guess each activity.

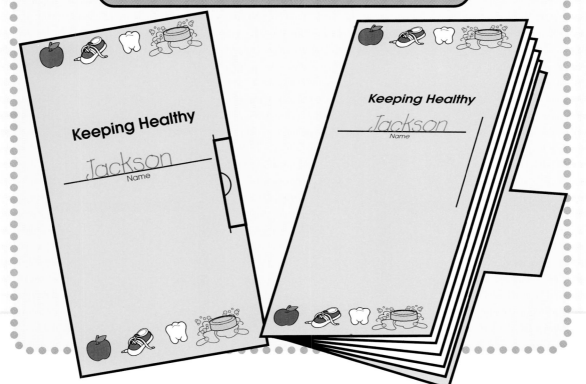

Booklet Cover

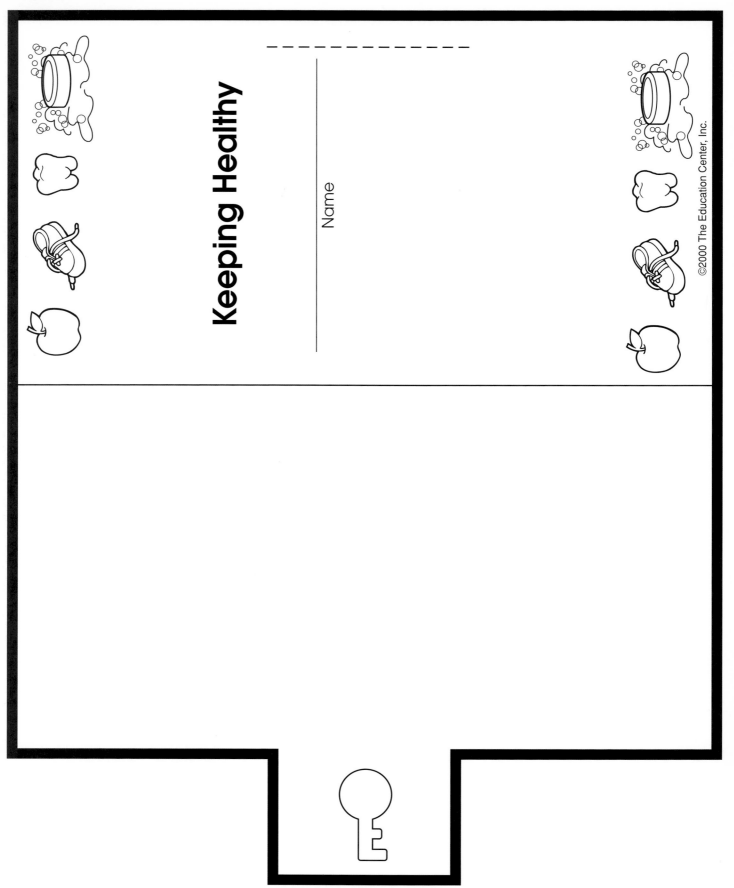

Keeping Healthy

Name

©2000 The Education Center, Inc.

©2000 The Education Center, Inc. • *I Can Make It! I Can Read It!* • *Spring* • TEC3507

90   **Note to the teacher:** Use with "Keeping Healthy" on page 89.

I wash my hands and face every day.

Monday   ☐ yes ☐ no

Tuesday   ☐ yes ☐ no

Wednesday   ☐ yes ☐ no

Thursday   ☐ yes ☐ no

Friday   ☐ yes ☐ no

2

I eat healthy food every day.

On Monday, I ate _____

On Tuesday, I ate _____

On Wednesday, I ate _____

On Thursday, I ate _____

On Friday, I ate _____

1

Note to the teacher: Use with "Keeping Healthy" on page 89.

Booklet Pages

I exercise every day.

On Monday, I _____

On Tuesday, I _____

On Wednesday, I _____

On Thursday, I _____

On Friday, I _____

4

I brush my teeth every day.

Monday ☐morning ☐night

Tuesday ☐morning ☐night

Wednesday ☐morning ☐night

Thursday ☐morning ☐night

Friday ☐morning ☐night

I go to the dentist to get my teeth cleaned.

☐yes ☐no

3

Note to the teacher: Use with "Keeping Healthy" on page 89.

I LOVE YOU!

Celebrate Mother's Day in heartwarming style with this priceless booklet! Invite each student to name things her mother (or another female caregiver) does that make her special. Record student responses on the chalkboard. Then give each student a copy of pages 95 and 96 and a construction paper copy of page 94. Read each booklet page with students. Help each student write her responses on booklet pages 1–3, encouraging her to refer to the responses on the chalkboard as needed. On booklet page 4, invite the student to draw a picture of her mother. Next, have her cut out her booklet cover and pages along the bold outer lines. Direct her to fold back her cover where indicated, stack her pages in numerical order, and place them inside the cover. Staple the booklet at the shoulders. Have the student address and sign her cover and then color it. When students have completed their booklets, provide time for each child to read hers to the class. Then encourage each student to take her booklet home to read and give to her mother. This personal booklet is sure to please!

CREATIVE DECORATING OPTIONS

- Glue paper doily pieces to the collar.
- Glue ribbon, buttons, and bows to the cover.

> To extend this booklet activity and celebrate the everyday things that moms do, read aloud *What Mommies Do Best* by Laura Joffe Numeroff (Simon & Schuster, 1998).

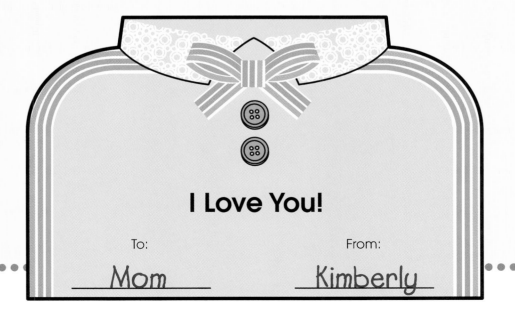

I Love You!

To: _____Mom_____   From: _____Kimberly_____

Booklet Cover

Fold.

I Love You!

To:

From:

_____

_____

Note to the teacher: Use with "I Love You!" on page 93.

Thanks for helping me

_____

– – – – – – – – – – – – – – – – – – – –

_____

_____

– – – – – – – – – – – – – – – – – – – –

_____

_____

– – – – – – – – – – – – – – – – – – – –

_____

1

I love it when you

_____

– – – – – – – – – – – – – – – – – – – –

_____

_____

– – – – – – – – – – – – – – – – – – – –

_____

_____

– – – – – – – – – – – – – – – – – – – –

_____

2

Note to the teacher: Use with "I Love You!" on page 93.

You make me feel special when you

_____

- - - - - - - - - - - - - - - - - - -

_____

- - - - - - - - - - - - - - - - - - -

_____

- - - - - - - - - - - - - - - - - - -

_____

3

Thanks for taking care of me. I love you!

4